Preface

This is a book, told by Ben, written by Ben, and loved by Ben. Sometimes, there were issues with the keyboard and the typist's chair. !!

We hope you enjoy the journey, and have fun reading this, his first book.

As his human Mum, I had to help a little, but the passion he gave to the story was brilliant.

Sometimes, he even talks to us. Clever dog, I think.

Acknowledgements

There are many humans to thank for help and love along the way. They know who they are.........Big thank you to all.

Animals next:

Love to: Jim, Brandy, Simba, Mac, Rosie, Max, Freddie and Jas.

Thank you all for being a large part of life on this planet.

We are sure that without having known and loved you all, our very being would have been compromised. Enjoy the story. I have to go now, as I am very hungry. Also, a trip to the park might be in the offing. !!!!!!!!!!!!!!!!!!!!!!!!!   xxxxxxxxx

The Start

Hi, I am called Ben, I am a German Shepherd Dog with a long coat, and one ear that never went up. I have a large black nose, that is always very wet and friendly. This is the first book that I have written. I wrote it a while ago, but other things got in the way. Hence, the delay. Here we are now:

I wrote the book four years ago, and it took a while, due to the fact I am not very good with the keyboard, or indeed sitting on a chair. I got there in the end, but it kind of got left on the desk in the office, until today. Lots of people spoke to my Mum about it, and said "Why not ?" Give it a go, nothing to lose except a little time. Voila..............................Here is the story.

I am a six year old German Shepherd Dog. I think there were six or seven of us, born in a council house in Chelmsford, Essex. My Birth Mother was lovely, but I think (I know) that I was the runt of the litter. About 4 weeks into my life, the human called Gail, brought this lady into the house. We were running around, ripping up furniture, as you do. The lady picked some of us up, and then turned to Gail and said "NO, we can't have a puppy" "No way, No how, Never" Damn, Why not ??? What's not to like. With that, the lady left.

Another four weeks passed, and then "Voila", I was being taken away to a family. These two teenagers has bought me for their Mum, as a surprise for Christmas. Their own Shepherd had died a few months before, and they thought that I would be the perfect surprise. I was ecstatic. New things to chew. I could not have been happier. They got me a big basket and toys and everything you could imagine. I was to be a complete surprise for their Mum.

A word : NEVER give animals of any kind as a surprise for Christmas. It is not fair, to the animal or the human.

I could hear this "new human Mum" on the telephone to a friend, saying what a lovely surprise, to have been given a new puppy the day before Christmas Eve, as a gift. How thoughtful the kids were, as she had lost her other dog, her husband had left her just after 9/11 for another woman, her own Dad had died, and now she had me to love. Confused ? Me too.

I cried myself to sleep that night, in my new basket. I was a Christmas present. I was a gift under the Christmas Tree.

How does that work ? It doesn't. I couldn't run away, being only a little over eight weeks old. I didn't have any money, a place to run to. I couldn't drive either (not old enough).

The tears were running down my nose, making my whiskers wet. I felt so sad and alone. I only wanted to chew furniture and have fun, and run and play.

If they had put me in a box and wrapped it with Christmas paper, it would have been no worse.

The next day, things happened……………………Frantic things.

I could hear the woman on the telephone, that morning. It was the 24th December 2002. I don't know who she was speaking to, but she was making arrangements to return me ? NO, not back with the rest of the litter. Oh God, not the litter again !

The woman made another call, and with that, bundled me into her car, with my new toys and basket. Where were we going ? I was very frightened, but just sat there quietly.

We stopped in front of a different house from where my life had started. I just hoped it wasn't a home for unwanted pets.

What a shock.

I was handed over to a couple. Me, just a tiny ball of fur.

I met my new humans. I still live with them. Someone was looking out for me that night.

I didn't realize that it was Christmas Eve, 2002.

Then, I saw him !!!!!!!!!!!!! He was a long haired German Shepherd Dog, and he was big. I mean really big.

He must have weighed near on 50 kilos. My goodness, shock or what ?

This was to be my new home, and I had to share with a dog that big !!!! Oh My God. What's a puppy to do? Maybe the litter was a better bet.

This couple just said "Max, meet Ben."

Big dog looked at me, our eyes met, and I knew that I was home.

Home at last.

Or, so I thought.

The couple said that I could stay for a while, just to see if I fitted in.

Well, being Christmas Eve, with friends arriving for lunch on Christmas Day, I quickly decided to fit in.

You would try to, wouldn't you ?

The next morning, they were unwrapping gifts, but I didn't have any. They gave me a couple of Max's toys to play with. New toys, that, he had been given for Christmas. That was nice and thoughtful of them.

My new human Mum, told me her name was Vonnie, and my new human Dad, told me he was Dean.

Vonnie called Max "Handsy". Strange, when his name was Max. I did learn later that it was short for Handsome, which he was. Well, I wasn't going to argue with him on that score !!

We had a wonderful Christmas Day, with friends arriving for lunch, and I appeared to be rather a novelty.

After that Christmas, I settled in rather well. I still had to be careful not to let Max roll on me, as he might have hurt me, being such a large friend.

One day spilled into another……………………….and I guess I was there to stay.   Yippee.

My new humans both worked, but we soon developed a routine.

Every morning we would go to the local park, and then again in the evening. At the weekends, we would go to a really big park in the car, which was great.

I always liked having two items to play with, and hold in my mouth, so I had one red rubber bone and one blue one. Max, he liked a large Frisbee, usually red. This was after he dropped his red ball, yellow ball in our fish pond, and they sunk !!

Max was a brilliant sportsman, and showed me how to run, jump and catch.

Then blow me down, something awful happened.

We were all playing in the local park one evening, and another dog tried to catch Max's Frisbee. He defended it, and the dog, called Poppy, bit him very badly on the side of his face. I was so frightened, that I ran and hid behind the kiddies swings. Took a lot of coaxing to get me back home.

I was so scared, but I couldn't help Max. This incident made me very wary, and from that day to this, I still dislike ALL other dogs. Max was my only friend.

We muddled along. My human Mum and Dad, (dare I call them Mum and Dad? Could I hope they would keep me ?), both went to work.

Whilst they were at work, I gradually ate my way through the house.

Max just used to watch me, which was quite funny. I think he thought that I was the unpaid entertainment.

I started with the telephone cables. Once you manage to get a real hold of the cable with your teeth, it's amazing how easy it is to pull the whole cable off of the wall. I did that twice !!

Another time, I ate the carpet on the stairs. I chewed the memory card for Dad's Playstation, which was really easy to pull out of the machine, strangely. I broke the TV cabinet, and even chewed both of their best rugs, at each end, which they had to get repaired. I knew when I chewed the foot stool and chased the filling around the lounge, it was the end of the story.

I couldn't help myself, I just couldn't.

It arrived as a flat pack.............................Excitement, as it was for me and only me.

Dad assembled it, with all of us watching. It was for me !!!

I could not wait to see what present I was to receive, AND then I realized...........................YEP, it was for me, and only me.

IT WAS A CAGE !!!!!!!!!!!!!!!!!!!!!!!!!!!!   A CAGE !!!!!!!!!!!!!!!!

In the lounge, there was a CAGE !!!!!!!!!!!!!!!!!!!

Max was sniggering in the background, so much so, he nearly fell over. I have never seen another dog laugh so much, the first time they put me in there.

I will say no more on the matter, except that it was a safe haven for me. I could not play with any household items ever again.

I had learned my lesson.

I still disliked other dogs though.

The routine was established. Me.........cage. Max.......smiling. Mum and Dad..............work.

The balance was established. The routine was wonderful.

Out in the garden, I still tried to get some fun going though. I could wind Max up so easily. I took him up to the fish pond one day. He had his red ball, yellow ball, in his mouth. I got him to look in at the fish, and guess what ?? He dropped both of them right into the pond. They were heavy rubber ball, and immediately sunk !!!!!!! He was mortified. The parents could not retrieve them, as the pond was deep. HAH !!!!!!!

Max then moved on to a Frisbee after the incident, but for some reason would only have a red one. What's that about ?

Max did have a girlfriend called Rosie, but she didn't like me, not even a little. I think that I may have been too small at the time, rather like the weasel I was. Anything I could do to have a laugh with Max, I would consider doing.

Great fun times.

Once, my parents decided to have a Summer House built in our garden. Construction began, and it was very exciting. The wiring was nearly complete, but not yet connected. In hindsight quite a good thing.

My indoor cage was getting a little snug, so when they were at work, they put me in the Summer House. Wiring is quite easy to remove, if you chew it all day. Enough said on that one. They did have to get the place re-wired. I did get used to my name that Summer.

BENNNNNNNNNNNNNNNNNNNNNNNNNN what have you done?

I did learn a few words that I had never heard before. What did they mean ?

BBBBBBBEEEEEEEENNNNNNNNNNNNNNNNNNN

What's a puppy supposed to do ?

Never say that you can get a camel through the eye of a needle.

I used to run the gauntlet of the flower beds. They looked so pretty. All newly planted, and so pretty, especially for Max to bury a pig's ear in. I bet the people that live in our old house are still digging up roasted pig's ears ! Sorry piggies x

He could dig, that boy.

We had a garden shed, next to a fence, with just enough space for me, being a puppy, to get through. I could do a decent lap around the shed, over the flower beds, and back, and then just repeat the process. I saw Max watching me, and then horror of horrors, he decided to give it a go. I knew he would have, and I was taunting him, just a little. He started off at a great pace, and then suddenly, between the shed and the fence, became stuck, yes stuck. Hard and fast. The big boy was stuck !!

I had led him into a trap. I was free, being a kid, but he was stuck fast. Hee hee.

I thought they were going to have to call the Fire Men.

Mum and Dad had to remove the contents of the shed, and then move the shed, to free Max. They told him off, but I could see from the look he gave me................he knew that I was to blame.

Happy Days x

Lots of fun, and loads of laughs, and the cage finally left the building.

THEN, dog training. I do not think so. Not me, I do not like other dogs, not one jot. Dog training ? What is that about ?

I am perfect. I am house trained. I walk on a lead, perhaps pull a little. I don't need to go to boot camp.

So, the man arrived at our house to assess me (WHAT ?) Why did I need assessing ? I did not like him one bit.

Has was an Ex Police dog trainer. I couldn't take to him, even though he was very good, apparently.

He took me out, gave me an assessment, and told my Mum that he thought I would benefit from some decent training. Ok,Ok, I pulled on the lead a little, but nothing bad. I still didn't like him. BUT…………the following week, off we go. We leave Max, home alone, to put his paws up.

How many dogs ???? Which one to bite first ???? No, I can't do that, there's too many. Lots of German Shepherd Dogs, and Newfoundland, couple of small Springers, a Lab. My goodness. I could have had a brilliant fight with one of them. Or a decent nip.

Too many, just too many.

We were in a big field. Such a selection, but WOOOAAAHHH Mind-blowing. Which way do I look, who is next to me. I was surrounded. No-one is listening to me. I have questions to ask, why weren't they listening ?

My Mum was busy trying to get me to sit, stay, stand, walk-on, leave, find, all with treats to encourage me. Only so many treats you can have, before you start to feel very sich.

I was exhausted, after a session lasting two hours. Two hours, I ask you. I needed some Rest and Relaxation. And we drove home with my rubber bones on the bonnet of her car. It was only at the Army and Navy roundabout that she realised, and had to jump out to bring them into the car. Could have lost both of them.

When we arrive home, she then takes the Big One out, down to the river for a long walk. Both of us, on a lead is too much for Mum to handle, so she takes us out one at a time. Makes sense, as I am getting bigger, and have to stay on the lead. Max can walk on his own !!

We suddenly settle into a great routine. Every week, I go training and try to learn new things.

(Hoping that you are enjoying this story so far, as things do indeed become more interesting)

So it's another Wednesday morning, and off we go. I have my wheels, my Mum, and my blue and red rubber bones, which I still have. We all meet up, and then BINGO, someone catches my eye. She is a small black and tan German Shepherd Dog, called Amber. I can see hearts, flowers and love. We pal up, and things seem really good. I settle down to the routine, with Amber by my side, and we seem to master most of the training thrown at us. I am really sad when it's time to go home, but I really look forward to the following week.

Everything does now seem to have purpose and a good routine. I tell Max about Amber, and my day. He isn't phased. I can only assume he has had more than one love in his life. He tells me that whilst I am away learning, her just zonks on his bed, having lovely dreams of the beach, and chasing things. Sniffing and fun times. All while I am working. Not fair.

I have also made another friend at the training. He is another large GSD called Beaudi, very handsome. My Mum and his Mum get on really well, especially if we go to the pub for a drink.

Next week, we are going for a long, long walk along something called a river. I don't know what that is, but sounds like fun. At least we don't have to sit, retrieve, etc etc.

The following week arrives, and it's called Monday morning. Parents do not seem happy about it. I don't know what it means, because every day is the same for myself and Max, with a few exceptions. What is Monday ?? Strange word. We only know, food, drink, walkies, car/van, wee wee, etc….. oh and play, fun time.

Wednesday quickly arrives, and we dress for the morning. It's a lovely warm Summer's day, and off we go. We leave Max at home "Yipping". That is a very high pitched noise, which for a large dog IS rather strange. It sounds like "yip, yip, yip, yip, yip, yip, etc forever. He does it in the car, all of the way anywhere, and then all of the way back. Long journeys, don't go there. I think it's the excitement and anticipation of the end of the journey, or maybe he has always been like that. He greets people with the "yip". He never growls, well only if I step over him, so I try not to. I heard my Dad say that Max is the Apha doggie, so am I the Beta doggie ? I digress, we leave Max "Yipping".

Of we go, of we go, to something called a river walk. Hopefully their will be food involved. I also get to see Amber again. If I smoked, I could have a quiet cigarette with Beaudi, when we get to the River thing.

We arrive at the venue, everyone greats each other, dogs and humans alike. I give Rod, the trainer, a sideways glance. How I would love to nip him, and he knows, because he gives me the same look, funny though.

Off we all go. Lots of countryside, loads of different smells. Everyone stopping to leave a p-mail and more. Great fun. Beautiful day, and no doubt it will get even better.

Smells, grass, flowers, walkers, and we turn a corner, and someone says "There's the river" !!!!!!!!!!!

It's water, and I need a drink. It's like a big bowl of water, and looks amazing on this very hot day. I have never seen so much water before in my life. I am thirsty and would love to drink it all.

We wander alongside this big water. Suddenly, as we are all off lead, some of them decide to jump in. How?? How can they do that. Is it safe ?? No, it's fine, when someone shouted they can swim, I didn't know what swim was. I have never tried to get in my water bowl at home. Beaudi makes a run at the river, and suddenly he can swim. Amber follows. My Mum says to me "Go, Ben, go swim" I jump from the bank, and guess what ? I can swim, I can really swim. I only did dog paddle, no fancy strokes, but it was really great. One small dog paddle for mankind !!! (dogkind)

It was such a great feeling, but I never thought I would do it, but I did. I put my whole head under the water, and then I couldn't breathe, which was really strange. I learned to do it without putting my head in the water, and it was great. We all had fun, and when we climbed out of the river, shook ourselves all over the humans. Amazing.

I continue every week with the training, and feel like one of the pack. I still do not like other dogs, or indeed cats, or birds, but at least I am learning.

Then, one day, I get spooked. I don't know why. I just ran away. Something, just something, spooked me. Still, Mum then took Max for a few weeks, and he "Yipped" so much, she had to give up. He "yipped" through every exercise, all the way there and back in the car. Mum was stressed. But, at least I didn't eat the house any more.

I had finally grown up, at the age of 2 years, and was nearly as big as Max..

The Middle

One night, when all was quiet, Max and I had just finished our dinner, and were snoozing in front of the fire. We were listening, kind of, to our parents talking about moving abroad. We looked at each other, with that look, you know that look. I could see what was running through Max's mind (same as mine), "Great, Australia"…………..Lovely beaches, swimming in the sea, and NO more rain. We gave each other a sideways glance.

Then were heard them say "France", we were moving to France !! FRANCE………….. Neither of us could speak French, we didn't like garlic, or snails, and worse still, we couldn't ride a bike, sell onions, and didn't own a beret between us !!!!!!!!! Mon Dieu !!!!!!!! My God, how were we going to survive ????

The plans were being mad. The house went on the market, and within a week, had an offer on it. Panic stations.

Our Dad was very busy at work, so he said to Mum "Go to France and find a house that we can all live in happily. Must have a large secure garden, edge of village, central heating and a decent roof. Dad being a roofer need to get the priorities in order.

Mum decided to take her Mum along (Grandma Pauline) for some moral advice, even though she wasn't a property tycoon, but at least it could be a nice beano for them. Maybe they wouldn't find a house. Who knows ?? We just kept smiling to each other, and rolling around on the floor. Dad would have his hands full for that week, whilst they were swanning around France, enjoying the food, wine and scenery, Dad had to walk, feed, water and poop scoop !!!!!!!

No, it wouldn't happen. This was surreal (whatever that means).

Next thing we heard, Mum had lined up appointments with local Estate Agents, flights and car hire were booked, and they were on the next flight out of England. Well, well.
Well, to cut a long story short. Mum and Grandma found a house, with a large garden, edge of a nice village, and a good solid roof. It also has central heating and an open fire in the lounge. Dad looked at the pictures, and said "Yes, looks fine to me". They paid the deposit and everything was set. Hopefully, our house in Essex would complete on the sale.

That was in March 2004. We had a great Summer, with a paddling pool in the garden, for Max and myself.

Friends arrived, and we had BBQ's. Good fun times. How would France compare with this love that we all received from family and friends ? We would be all alone, just the four of us in a strange country, surrounded by French people. We would never have any friends again. We were leaving them all behind, and I felt sad. I never told Max, because he was too laid-back to worry about anything like that. As long as he had a car to go out in, and a Frisbee, nothing seemed to bother him.

ME, I worried for the two of us. I couldn't sleep, I just kept worrying. Would they put us on an airplane, and who would meet us at the other side. Would we go on a boat ? So many questions that I couldn't ask Mum and Dad.

Maybe the house sale would fall through, and we could stay in our house in Essex, with everything familiar.

I even went off of my food. Hard to imagine, I know.

Things then went quiet, so nothing to worry about.

Suddenly.............................contracts on our house were exchanged, and we were going.

That was at the beginning of June 2004. We were leaving. We couldn't move to France to get our new house until the 1st July.

Our furniture and belongings were packed up, and put into storage until they were delivered to France, and we moved into a friend's small house, for a month. Thank you Sue, because we had a small garden. It was a little snug, but at least we were all together, and there was a park, and Dad stopped work for that month.

Max and I heard them talking about a ferry. What is a ferry? I know furry, but ferry?

Oh, but hang on, we weren't going on a furry ferry. We were going through a tunnel. What is that like the tunnel at the railway station ? I was a little confused about that. Still, Max was smiling in the background, and yipping sometimes.

The plan...............so I gathered, was that Mum and my Auntie Carole were to go on the furry ferry from Portsmouth to St. Malo, in France in my Mum's jeep.

Dad, and Max and I, and Uncle Steve, would load up Dad's van and go from England to France under the water, through a long tunnel on a train. That sounds OK. At least they would be with us both for the whole journey. They would then have around a six hour drive to arrive at our new village in France.

I finally got my nose, paws and whiskers around the plan.

Better, than putting us on a plane.

Another round of packing and planning, and then the day arrived. The 30th June 2004. We were set.

They went out for a pub lunch, leaving us home alone.

Max noticed that all of our food and treats were in large tins in the lounge, to be packed into the van. Surely they must have dog treats in France ? If they don't, what will we do ? Not sure about this.

Ever the clever one, Max, managed to nudge the top tin, and it fell open. Guess what? It was full of pig's ears. There must have been 20 of them.

What's a dog to do? Clever boy, Max.

By the time they returned from their Beef and Ale pies, there were only 2 left. FUN or what ?

Mum threw a fit. ""What about the journey to the tunnel, and then all the way from Calais ?" They will be so sick. One can only presume that she intended to say, sick as dogs. Did feel slightly squiffy, but didn't let on.

Dad was cool. He just said "They'll be fine". Max was grinning from ear to ear, and yipping.

And the adventure continued…………………………………..

With that…we set off to a place unknown to us. Quite an adventure, for two rescue dogs.

We did feel a little queasy, but didn't say anything to Dad and Uncle Steve. We didn't want to worry them, as they had to concentrate on the driving. Strange that tunnel thing. We thought that you actually drove through the tunnel in the van, from England to France, but they put you on a type of train thing. Then you eat sandwiches and have a cup of tea. Nice though, because we had company, and they made sure that we were fine.

We slept most of the way, as it was nearly midnight when we got to the tunnel. Dad drove through the night, with Uncle Steve giving directions. We stopped a few times, which enabled us to have a decent sniff (French scent), and go to the toilet. All in all, a very nice little trip. At least Max stopped yipping.

We arrived at our destination, very early the following morning. Mum and Auntie Carole were just getting off of the ferry at St. Malo, so had to drive for an hour to meet with us all.

Hooray, we met up as planned, in the local park, by the lake. It was lovely to see Mum again, and indeed Auntie Carole.

We apparently had to wait all day, because the house signing was at 4.0 pm, so we couldn't get the keys until then.

Mum went and got us some French bread and wine, and some cheese. (YUK – it didn't smell that great) No doubt, we would have to get used to this type of food. At least, it wasn't escargot in garlic !!!!!!!!! It was a hot day, with true blue sky, and wall to wall sunshine. We had a lovely picnic by the lake, and had arrived in heaven.

This was the beginning of a new adventure for us, as a family, and we couldn't stop smiling.

Mum and Dad went to the Notaire's office to sign for the house, and we stayed outside with Uncle Steve and Auntie Carole. They emerged after an hour or so, and off we went, back into the village with the keys to our new house.

When we arrived outside, Uncle Steve said "It's looks like the house from AmittyVille horror...." Never heard of that ?? Max and I sniffed around the house, checked out our lovely big garden, and we even had our own room !! From that day to this, it's always been called "The Boys Room". Don't know why, as we didn't have a bar or even a pool table. But, we always had our beds in there.

Job done. Now, we have to learn French. In hindsight, easier said, than done.

The routine, after Uncle and Auntie returned to England, was, and still is. Mum and Dad have a cup of tea, and we go to the park, play games, and have a long walk. The weather doesn't matter, we just go there and have fun. But we have a lovely garden to run in, and chase cats. We are winners, and it was brilliant.

Our Dad is a builder, and had to set up his business. This was great fun................not for him, but for Max and myself. Mum and Dad were painting the house, inside and out. Whilst doing this, they listened to endless CD's, read lots of books, and we could hear them practicing their French. Sounded like a different language to us, but it was. They battled on, which was really funny.

That Summer, in 2004, we had endless streams of visitors from England, even though we were in a muddle. Max and I loved the attention, though, and the treats given. Also, lots of phone calls and e-mails from friends and family. I bet they miss all of them.

OK. It's time to start work, for Dad. Registration complete, and even Uncle Steve and Auntie Carole over, to buy a house. Uncle Steve also registers for work, so Dad and Uncle can help each other out.

Enquiries start coming in, pricing for work, and things are hectic. Good, that means we can all eat !!

What's shopping ? I just hear Mum say, "OK boys, I'm going shopping". Then she appears with lots of bags. Doesn't always look like food to me, though.

We get into a routine………..Long walk after breakfast, then Mum does some paperwork, phone calls etc. We just laze around, snoozing in our room. Mum then decides to clean the house (seems like every day !!). There does seem to be mud and fur everywhere, but we don't care. Max just loves biting the vac. I join in, I don't know why, just because I can. He chases it around the house. He's the same with a broom and the lawnmower. I pretend, and just humour him. Xx

Christmas arrives, and then departs, having unwrapped, looked at our lovely gifts, we settle back in. This is just so laid-back, and we do smile at each other from time to time. Heaven x

Family and friends come and go, and the decorations are taken down. Everything is to go in the cupboard, until next Christmas. Mum packs the tree up, and leaves it at the bottom of the stairs, just taking the decorations upstairs, to return for the tree. She has taped the tree up, ready for it to go back into it's box. We didn't have a real tree, because of the needles. They got in our pads one year, and would had to have a bit of tweezer treatment. I always thought that needles were a metal item that you put cotton through, and stitched with. Different type of needle on a Christmas tree, I suppose, as there wasn't any metal, or cotton.

Mum takes the decorations upstairs, and the phone rings. I ran upstairs to help her answer it, and so did Max. Next minute, a big crash, and a big yelp. Max got half way up the stairs, and fell backwards. He was negotiating the turn, and slipped on the wood. Luckily he fell onto the tree at the bottom of the stairs. It must have cushioned his fall, thank goodness. You could see the marks on the stairs, and still can to this day. He was very lucky, not to have broken his back.

Mum ran downstairs, and told him off. Why..........he only wanted to help.

He always slept at night, in our room, downstairs, but every morning, he would come upstairs to round them up, for toast, and then the lovely walk.

He never, ever tried to go upstairs again.

That incident must have scared him so much.

So, instead of Max running around the bedroom "yipping", he used to encourage me to round them up. Very, very cunning, was Max !!

That was January 2006, and no harm done.

In the April, my Dad's brother and wife, and their two teenage children came to visit for a long weekend.

That's FOUR people for me to growl at !! I just didn't know which one to go for first. WOW

I'll be honest. When they arrived, they seemed very nice, so I just left them to it.

Mum said "Just ignore the boys", and they did. They ate dinner, didn't stroke either of us, no treats, NOTHING !

I thought, a plan would be, wait until they go to bed, and I can sneak into their rooms and lightly nibble (bite) them on at a time. No such luck !! Mum and Dad slept downstairs with us both, just to keep an eye on things. I didn't even get a slight chance to have a nibble.

One afternoon, we all decided (with the outlaws........that's Dad's family) to go for a long walk. I think I had a muzzle on, just in case we met other dogs. We walked for miles and miles.

SUDDENLY, Max collapsed.

Oh My God, we were a long from home, on foot. What could we do ?

I couldn't really help, especially with a muzzle on. Dad decided that the only thing for it, was to pick Max up, and carry him home. He carried him all of the way back. HOW ??

Max weighed around 46 kilos. (I had this information from the vet..........when our passports were renewed.) Pet Passports, not the human ones. The vet said that Max was over weight, so he had already lost 3 kilos, luckily for Dad.

Guess What ??? Dad did it. He carried Max all of the way home. We couldn't believe it. The outlaws couldn't, either !

It's a good job that Dad was strong......................years of training and hard work.

We arrived home safely, and were watered and fed. Max was none the worse for wear, the following day, which was a big relief.

After the family left for England, an appointment was made with our local vet, just to see what was going on.

I went along too. It's a ride out in the van, and maybe a treat was in the offing.

I stayed in the van, and Mum and Dad took Max in. He was "yipping" for the attention that the vet would give him.

They spoke on the way home about possibilities. Maybe a nerve problem in his back, or hip problems, or maybe nothing serious. It might have been from the fall on the stairs. They were quite upbeat about things, so we didn't worry. Then we had a pig's ear each, when we arrived home. Max could walk OK, so it went to the back of my mind. He could walk and run, and eat and drink, so life was good.

Summer arrived early. It was such a lovely time, and just to feel the sun on your back, have a roll around on the lawn, lovely. We had Barbeques, and drinks on the terrace. (How's that for an Essex couple.............I say couple, because, I am from Chelmsford, and Max from Dagenham) He has a pedigree though, I don't. Never mind, it matters not (well only to me).

I never wanted to join the Police Force, go and work abroad with the Army, or be a Guide Dog. I wanted to be myself. Don't get me wrong, though, the above are all very worthwhile careers, but barking and nibbling just seems better, somehow.

April rolled into May, and May into June, and yes, you've got it, SUMMER was here. It felt good. We could just snooze on the terrace, chase the birds in the garden, smell the BBQ cooking. The evenings were light and warm. Heaven on earth for everyone. YIPPEE !!!!!!!!!!!!!!!!!!!!!!!!!!!!!

But, something happened. Something was wrong............

Something bad...............YES...............something very bad.

The End

Max starts limping. He isn't able to chase Mr Frisbee without falling over. He can't run. He just keeps stumbling over.

I hear Mum and Dad talking.

Yet, another appointment, with the Vet.

This is not going well. I don't know what to do to help.

They left for the Vet's. When they were there, our Dad suggested a double hip replacement operation. She said it would cost an awful lot of money. Thousands of Euros, which we didn't have, but Max would probably die during the operation. This was due to the fact, that he was nearly 11 years old. Also, the fact that he was quite a heavily built GSD. The breed went against him, as this problem is very common.

Alternatives ????????????

The Vet suggested two injections of cortisone into the back left leg, only, as the back right leg was fine. The injections would be very painful, and expensive. They went for it. Max didn't have an option.

You would have to try and make things better, wouldn't you ?

It may have made a marginal difference, possibly. I don't know, not being a Vet.

He was still as keen as ever, though, just limped very badly. He took his left back nails down to the quick, whenever he walked on a hard surface. He always cleaned them very thoroughly though. I was heartbroken.

Mum and Dad gave him strong painkillers, every day, and any supplement they could find, on the Internet.

My Mum did research, and talked to others that had experienced the same problem, with their doggies. I just got on with my own little life. Suddenly, I grew up......................

I know, I know............but I had to grow up, be the Man dog of the family.

Summer was here…………lovely. Max and I could just lay around on the lawn, watching Mum gardening. It was joyous.

AND THEN……………………………It arrived…………..

It was a chariot, for Max. But we had a car and a van, and they had a couple of bicycles !!!!!!!!!!!!!! This was interesting.

Mum and Dad bought it off the Internet, from the USA. They had to give very precise measurements of Max. Paid their money, and it was delivered.

Max did NOT like the look of that thing. Every time they brought it into the garden, he ran (limped) away. I didn't like the look of it, either. It was like a dog wheelchair. That's how bad things were. We had to put a 50 kilo Max in a wheelchair.

But, thinking about it. Not such a bad idea. I leave the thought with you.

Christmas came, and then went. Max was relying more and more on constant care, both at home at when we went to the park. No-one could make it better, sadly.

Mum's friend, Sue, arrived in the April, and by then, Max was dragging himself around. He couldn't chase the Frisbee, unless he was in the chariot. We carried on, because we had to.

Mum and Dad slept downstairs on the sofa bed, just to keep things calm, and be there to take care of Max. I stayed with them all, to help look after my best friend. My best friend in the whole world was really ill, and I had to be there for him.

Grandma visited, and I heard her say to Mum "If you treat me, as well as you treat Max, when I can't get about, then I'll be happy". No contest, Grandma.

For one, Grandma is not that furry, she doesn't have a large black, wet nose, and she is a human !!!!!!!!!!

I remember that Max started to lose a little body function. Just from time to time, he may have a little wee-wee on the floor. The vet said "He's incontinent". I remember thinking.......but we live in a continent ! I misunderstood.

Mum started buying waterproof under pads for our bed, just to help the situation.

They never took us to the vet's surgery............just too stressful. They just went to discuss matters.

I did in fact go to the Vet in the June, to get my pet passport renewed, but Max didn't go with me. Maxie boy stayed home. Mum and Dad knew that his time was running out.

It brings a lump to my throat to even think about it. Darling Max, my big brother.

I still carried on at the park, chasing my red and blue rubber bones. Every time we went to the park, Max came along on his chariot, with the Frisbee. We went in Dad's van, and Max would run and catch. Sometimes, he would tip the chariot over, and Mum and Dad would have to pick him up, and off again.

Even the French would give a cheer when they saw him running on his wheels.

Both of Max's back legs had gone, so he needed constant care. A lot of planning to get him round the garden. The chariot was too big (even though, very light) to bring into the house, so he had to rely on care from Mum and Dad.

NEVER, EVER, was there any talk of putting Max to sleep. NEVER, for as long as it took, they would keep him going. If he wanted to give up, then, that would be the time. He didn't give up. He still loved life, and the attention. He was still "yipping" in the van, when we went out.

Unfortunately, this is the real end. Totally, the end.

On a very warm day in August, Mum and Dad decided that we should go to the beach. Just because, it was a beautiful day, and the sand and salt water, and the waves……………..just so much fun. I remember, it was a Monday…………..

We could not find a dog friendly beach, as it was the height of the holiday season. We came home, very disappointed.

Dad hosed both Max and myself down in the back garden to make up for the disappointment, and then set a BBQ.

Our parents decided to try again on the Wednesday. And we found the perfect beach, and I ran and ran, chased my bones, and drank so much salt water !!! Max was on his wheels with his Frisbee, and it was wonderful. We paddled, and life was great. Nice and warm. We slept all of the way home. Just dreaming of chasing…….cats, bones, Frisbees. Lovely.
I'll pass you over to my Mum. She can tell you more xx

Hi, it's Ben's human Mum, Vonnie.

The day at the beach was wonderful. The boys ate their dinner, and we did indeed have a BBQ.

On Saturday the 11th August 2007, Dean was called out for an emergency plumbing job. We then went to a BBQ at some friends, in the afternoon. We didn't stay long, as we needed to get back home for Max.

If he needed to go out in the garden, we would lift his poor back legs, to let him go to the toilet.

His spirit was great. We just hoped that he wouldn't get worse. Ben , also, just wanted to keep his best friend.

We hoped.

Ben prayed.

We prayed.

The Sunday (12th August 2007), was lovely and sunny, so Max and Ben could be outside in the garden. We just chilled, and they both had a great day. Nothing seemed any worse. We knew it couldn't get better. If it had stayed the same, we would have coped with it all.

Monday 13th August 2007.

At around 5.00 am, Max called.........................It was just a quiet "Yip Yip". I went into the boy's room. Max was just lying there, his teeth clenched, and looking, very poorly. I tried to give him a drink, from that little porcelain bowl, that he favoured. Strange, how when we had to give a drink to him, because he couldn't get up to drink, he would only drink from that bowl, never the stainless steel "boys" bowl.

I called Dean, we took turns to get dressed and look after Max. The sun was rising, and the temperature looked good for the day. We drank tea, many cups of tea, just looking at the garden.

We both knew that this was the end of a journey, for all of us.

Max was rescued, and given to us, when he was three years old. When he was six years old, we took Ben, as a puppy. They were best friends.

Laying their with the door open, Dean said to Max "Look at the sky, Maxie". It was just so sad. Big, fluffy and noble, so laid back in life, he was even noble at the end.

Ben cleaned Max's face, for the final time.

Ben can now take over, because, this is, his book.

OK, OK. Mum wrote the last piece, but it didn't mean that I couldn't. I just could not find the right words.

Max was a master of play, and all things funny. He was upright and proper. He had a long coat, and two ears that stood up straight. Also, he had a pedigree.

Me, dodgy ear, one eye smaller than the other, and large odd front feet. Didn't matter. He loved me.

I have now become slightly more tolerant of people and other dogs. I will never, ever, be cat friendly. Just my way.

Max taught me many tricks, and in turn, I taught him many. Two way street, that I miss.

On that day, Mum and Dad waited until Uncle Steve arrived at 8 o'clock in the morning. Dad explained that he wouldn't be going to work that day, as we had to go to the vet.

Dad and Uncle Steve carried Max to Dad's van, on his bed. Mum sat in the back with Max. She stroked his head all of the way to the vet.

From what I know, as I stayed home, they carried Max into the clinic, and our vet, put Max to sleep, on that sunny morning in August.

I couldn't quite understand why they arrived home without him, but they tried to explain to me. I still expect him to walk through the door, to this day.

I think Mum and Dad had a few glasses of wine that sunny day.

Life would never be the same again, for the family.

Thank you for your understanding. It has been difficult for me to write this book, as I am not an author. First book, for me.

I hope that you have enjoyed it.

Yours Ben …………………(Mr Wonderful)

PS. Why was Max called Handsy (Handsome), Me – Mr Wonderful, and our Dad (wait for it) BUBBLES………..!!!!!!!!!!!!!!!!!!!!!!!??????????????????

What planet is our Mum on !!!   ????

Hee hee xx

Mum sent letters and e-mails to friends, to tell them, about Max. The first is Mum's e-mail, and following are the replies received. The e-mail addresses have been deleted, but the names are genuine.

E-mail from Dean and Von.

Header. Max – 5th July 1995 – 13th August 2007.

Hi from both of us.
We are sorry to tell you that we had to have Max put to sleep, yesterday morning.
He started to lose the use of his left back leg, last summer, and we sent to the USA for a tailor-made chariot.
He was not best pleased.
After a while, his right back leg started to go, and then we used the wheels, for walks, chasing Frisbee., etc.
Obviously, it has been a very difficult year for us all, but we coped. Max was always bright and happy.
Unfortunately, over the past few months, he became worse, but we soldiered on, as did Max.
He was quite demanding, calling for a drink, to be moved, or turned over. We nursed him 24/7, and now Dean and I have nothing to do.
He was a great character, larger than life itself, and very handsome. (Yes, Sue Donald, the Brad Pitt of dogs) !!
Sorry to tell any of you again, that may already know.
Love Von and Dean xx
PS. We took both Ben and Max to the beach on Wednesday, for a last paddle together.

We received many replies. Again, I will show them as received.

"To Dean and Vonnie,
We all are sorry to hear about Max, our thoughts are with you both. All our love, Gillian, Andrew, Sandra, Carlotte, James and Samuel xx "

"Hi Von and Dean,

I am so sad to receive this news…what a difficult year for you both, and for Max. It will take a while to recover, also because without all of the nursing, he will leave an even bigger void behind………
I will tell Marco about Max. Stay close..allow yourselves some quiet time…..
Lots of love, Martina"

"Dear Von and Dean,
I am so sorry for you losing Max. It made me cry. I know exactly how you are feeling, as we lost Rosie in March. They are a part of your life, and make such an impact. Just Remember the good times and what you all shared together.
I do hope that you are both OK, and am so gutted we didn't meet up. Charlie wanted to meet Max again.
Please be strong and smile when you think of him.
Love always, Sam, Blue and Charlie xx
PS Sorry for the delay, only just checked my e-mails."

"Thank you for the photo. Bless him. Max really was a big handsome dog, and I know he was your baby. As well as mourning his passing, try, if you can to celebrate his life and wear a smile, for him.
Tony and Lisa."

"Hi,
So sorry to hear your sad news. We know what it's like, having
to make that decision, as we did with Jodie, last year. We all
blubbered at the time. I expect Ben will miss him as much as
you do, having grown up, always having him there. Keep
looking at that lovely photo you sent, and think of all of the good
times.
Love Barry and Liz."

"Hello both,
Sorry to hear about the loss of Max. Although we did not meet
him, he does look a character, in the photo. Apart from the
obvious sadness, we hope that you are both well, and still
enjoying life in Brittany.
Good to hear from you, although probably not the best time for
you.

Love and Best Wishes, Steve and Liz."

"Dear Vonnie and Dean,
Just arrived home from work, and your e-mail had me reaching
for the tissue box again. What a fabulous photo of the "old boy".
He certainly did have a very handsome look about him, and it is
so sad that he is no longer with you. But, he will always be in
your hearts (and mine too), with loads of happy memories.
How is Ben coping without his mate.....I guess this must seem
very strange to him also. I imagine it mush feel like a part of you
is missing, and will take time to get used to.
If you need someone to talk to, give me a call. You know you are
always in my thought. Love you both, loads Sue xxx"

"Hi Von and Dean,
We are so sorry to read about Max, but you did the right thing.
It was nice that you went to the beach on Wednesday. We did
this same with Chester, my Mum's dog, on his last few day.
Love to you all, Sue and Brad"

"Sorry to hear your sad news about Max...I know exactly what
you're going through, it does get better though ! That was a
lovely picture of him on your e-mail. I felt he was a bit hairy for
Brad Pitt !!! More of a Brian Blessed !!! Only joking. He was a
handsome chap !
Hope to hear from you soon, when things are a bit chirpier....it
will happen !!
Lots of Love, Kim xx!

"Sorry to hear of your loss. Max.....he was a great dog, and he
fell on his feet, when you chose him. Lucky dog, and a lovely
picture of him. I still have a few pictures from dog "Training".
Grace (their dog) is still captain of the boat, but we have the boat
up for sale, and are hoping to buy a motor home, so we can see a
bit of Europe. Who knows, we may pass your way !!
Will chat soon, Lots of Love, Sue, Rick and Grace xxx"

"Dear Dean and Von,
So sorry to hear your news about Max. We are sure he is in a
good place, with loads of cats, and Frisbees to chase all day long.
And no discomfort. Love Mike and Lorraine x"

"Dear Von and Dean,

So sorry to hear about Max – I must admit, I had a little cry. Beaudi is nearly 12 years old now, and his arthritis is pretty bad, but he seems fairly healthy otherwise. He complains, but that seems to go with the male sex, as they get older ! (other text) Anyway, write when you can. I get a bit lonely out here, and once again, sorry about Max (I shall keep his photo) Love,Joan and Beaudi x"

"Dear Von, Thanks ever so much for your card and letter. So sorry to hear about Max. Just remember he had a good life with a family, who loved him. (other text) Take care, Love to Dean, as well as you, Kim x"

(All of the comments above, were taken from true extracts of letters and e-mails received)

Thank you everyone, for all of your kind comments, and thoughts. I must admit, for the first time in four years, I have read every single one of them once more, and cried, again.

Thank you.

The Final Journey

We are on our way. The final journey will start.
Before, the journey begins……………..Mum and Dad gave the
chariot on loan to another couple, here in France. They have a
holiday home, and their German Shepherd, Luke, is suffering
the same problem. They didn't like to ask, but after Max left us,
two weeks later, they asked. So, the chariot went to another.

Luke's family used it for two years, taking it back to England
with them. We were quite happy for someone else to have fun
with it.

Sadly, we received an e-mail after that time, to say that Luke has
passed away, and that the chariot would come back to us.

We still have it, to this day. One day, hopefully, it will help
another. Xx

Back to…………The Final Journey.

Mum collected Max's ashes from our vet. We did keep them
here with us for a few months. Then, they decided to take them
back to England, and lay them with Simba's ashes, and indeed
Mum's Dad's ashes.

Euro tunnel booked……….me with my very own passport.

We made the journey back. Sad little threesome, in Dad's van.

We arrived at the church yard, and they had the ashes and glasses and champagne. You've guessed.

They opened the champagne, shared with Grandma Pauline, and Auntie Shirl, who, met us at the Church.

We toasted Max, as he arrived back to the village where Mum first met him. Leaden Roding, Essex.

The champagne was consumed, and the ashes scattered in memory of a very good friend, and loyal companion.

I never had any of the champagne, only a bowl of water, but I did take part in the moment.

It wasn't a sad moment, as Mum and Dad had been through so much, just looking after our every need.

Max was home, with Simba, and Grandad Eric.

R.I.P. sweet Max……………………….Miss you xxx

Max

Mummy's View

Hi, Just a few quick words from me. Not my book, it's Ben's.

I am indeed his human Mum.

He was a very difficult puppy, as being the runt of the litter, he was shoved around. This made him want to be the centre of attention.

He started from day one, sleeping on his back, with his leg's in the air, and still does, to this day.

This is very amusing for a dog of his size.

He has always needed two toys, in his mouth at any one time, and often stole items, if he only had one toy !!

He ate his way, through our house, and then one day, he grew up.

There was never, ever a thought to give him up.

He never touched Max's toys or food, because Max was the Alpha male. He would never step over Max, either.

Upon growing older, the "boys" as we called them, used to clean and groom each other. They got along really well. Having a new pup, made Max go back to being a pup again, which was really funny to see.

We did think, after Max left us, that Ben would go into decline, but although being the quieter of the two, he suddenly became very independent and loving.

I never realised, how much we gave to Max, in attention, because of his failing health. Looking after his every need, there was never enough time to give to both of them.
Towards the end, when Max couldn't stand unaided, he would only drink from his little china bowl. He would call for water, and we had to hold the bowl and give a drink. His whiskers would tickle your hand as your were holding the bowl !!

We did start to call Max, "Your Majesty".

The chariot became invaluable for daily walks in the park, and Max could still chase his Frisbee. At least both of the boys could have focus for that time every day.

I planned my day. Always, dealing with everything in the morning, getting home for lunchtime, and spending the afternoons, looking after Max, and indeed Ben.

Difficult times, but worth it for Max, we are sure.

We hope that you have enjoyed the book, and I cannot take any of this away from Ben. He wrote it, I only assisted in any way that I could. Thank you so much for reading it.

(Ben's Human Mum – Vonnie)

20741252R00026

Made in the USA
Charleston, SC
23 July 2013